MEDITATIONS FOR DAILY LIVING

K. ROBINSON

authorHOUSE®

AuthorHouse™
1663 Liberty Drive
Bloomington, IN 47403
www.authorhouse.com
Phone: 1-800-839-8640

First published by AuthorHouse 1/26/2011

ISBN: 978-1-4567-2643-0 (e)
ISBN: 978-1-4567-2642-3 (sc)

Printed in the United States of America

Also by Katrina Robinson

BOOKS

War For Your Dreams

War For Your Dreams Devotional

War For Your Dreams Journal

Poverty to Potential

CD's

Worship CD, 2011

TABLE OF CONTENTS
(List your favorites in order)

PEACE

The search for peace is coming from the inside out. Without even thinking, my mind searches for peace and pleasant ways to escape chaotic situations. A life without peace is a life without rest. My choices affect how much peace I will experience. I cannot sow seeds of chaos and expect to reap peace. *Lord, help me to make right choices and anticipate an abundance of peace.*

THOUGHTS

LONELINESS

Today if I feel lonely, I will not let it rule me. My feelings of abandonment and rejection will not last always. Pain is a part of living. Learning to digest it comes with time. Learning how best to ease it, comes with experience. This silent shadow requires divine intervention. God has to reach me in a place where no person can. People are human and full of flaws. They are not to be entrusted to bring healing in this area of my life.

Lord, heal me.. wholly and completely.

THOUGHTS

JEALOUSY

In my heart, I know jealousy lives. It causes me think bad thoughts about people I don't even know. It takes me into a world of fantasy. It causes me to compete with others. It causes me to see myself in terms of other people. I'm haunted by intimidation. Copycat is my middle name. *Lord, jealousy is responsible for my hidden fantasy world and negative behaviors.* Help me to create and accept a reality that brings me peace.

THOUGHTS

SELF-ESTEEM

My environment impacts the way I see myself in so many ways. The words people say, the things they do, even their point of view, has touched my confidence. The positive things make me feel relevant. The negative things send me into emotional turmoil. Neither should have control of my worth and value. *Lord, help me to have a balanced view of outside influences.* Let me find ultimate joy in who you created me to be.

THOUGHTS

PROBLEMS

My pockets are empty...
Utility company won't give me more time...
I lost my job...
The kids need clothes and shoes...
My mother is on drugs...
There's no health insurance...
I'm depressed....
Lord, handle all things that I can't. Grant me peace. And
if all things are well with me, than let me pray for
someone who is in distress.

THOUGHTS

LONGSUFFERING

Suffering is something I don't want to do. *Often, I feel like I've gone through enough.* Being patient, doing without, taking a second seat, or waiting for my time to be blessed is against my nature. Longsuffering is needed in every area of my life: home, church, work, and on the social scene. Going too fast will cost me too much.

Lord, help me to wait, be paced, and trust you.

THOUGHTS

JOY

My desire is to experience joy in everything. I don't want to be angry or pessimistic every waking moment. Life hasn't been easy, but replaying bad memories, keep me unhappy. Playing the victim does not last always. *Lord, give me joy…happiness that endures through good and bad times.* Help me to smile in adversity.

THOUGHTS

GREED

Sometimes, I think being rich would solve all my problems. *"If I just had more money, things would be so much better."* Happiness dependent upon bank account size is not happiness. That mindset is a greed trap. Some wealthy individuals are very unhappy. Money does not buy good health, love, or loyalty. *Lord, don't leave me blind.* Let me see that money will not solve every problem in my path.

THOUGHTS

MEDITATION

Solitude can be a wonderful thing. My space does not always have to be occupied. Noise is not necessary for me to find comfort. Sweet silence leaves my thoughts uninterrupted by the technological age we live in. It gives me the chance to evaluate, remember, and contemplate. My future depends on it. *Lord, help me make time to keep silent and meditate.*

THOUGHTS

CREATIVITY

I was born with gifts and talents. I'm not sure if I know what they all are. Exploring new avenues of creativity will help me discover them. Taking new challenges, finding new activities, and making new friends will reveal even more. *Lord, give me the desire to uncover the totality of who I am and what I can do.* Help me to overcome inward obstacles…including fear.

THOUGHTS

U.G.L.Y.

UGLY is not a bad word…

U.

G. otta

L. ove

Y. ourself

Lord, I accept how you have created me. Help me to see myself through your eyes.

THOUGHTS

PATIENCE

I am in need of patience. I need to be kind and courteous toward others. Patience builds my character. That' s what increases my value as a person: respect, integrity and compassion. *Lord, I need more patience so I can both earn respect from*

others, and give respect to others.

THOUGHTS

FEAR

There are so many things I'm afraid of. I'm afraid that my life will never change. I'm afraid of losing my friends. I'm afraid of being abandoned. I'm afraid of being without a job. I'm afraid of success. I'm afraid of failure. I'm afraid of change. I'm afraid of the future. I'm afraid of people. I'm afraid of sacrifice. I'm afraid of happiness. I'm afraid of shame. *Lord, only you can deliver me from FEAR*. Please deliver me!

THOUGHTS

INTEGRITY

I don't need to make vows or commitments that I cannot honor. I don't need to tell any tales, willfully pay bills late, or sign on the dotted line unless I am in agreement with the terms. "No" is not a dirty word. I should not have to be chased in order to be accountable. Hiding from responsibility is not an option. *Lord, help me to face my obligations and not make any unnecessary ones.*

THOUGHTS

LONELINESS

Today, loneliness is overtaking my mind and emotions. I feel like nobody in the world cares about me. My only escape is through drugs, alcohol, or false hope in relationships. I know those things never work, but they provide a quick fix, for a deep void. If I look too closely at my circumstances, I'll feel hopeless; even close to suicidal. *Lord, let me remember that if nobody else cares, you care.* Help me experience your personal touch.

THOUGHTS

SELF ESTEEM

It's tough sometimes to see the light at the end of the tunnel. There are days I feel so insignificant. When I feel bad about myself grooming, rest, and relaxing don't seem like good priorities. It's much easier to sulk and leave my life in total disarray. I have to remember that there is only one *me*. *Lord, help me to care about my personal being in the midst of feeling inadequate and sad.*

Please boost my energy, confidence, and self-worth.

THOUGHTS

TIME

Time is one of my most valuable assets. It is *non-refundable* and *non-transferable*; I need to use it wisely. There are many distractions to divert my attention from fulfilling responsibilities and obligations. Time will get past me and compound into years, if I'm not watching. *Lord, help me to track my time.* Show me how to streamline internet, T.V., and leisure hours to fulfill obligations to family, church, home, and myself.

THOUGHTS

ANGER

Although I'm angry, I don't have to let it control me. It is an emotion; one that can be managed. I won't allow it to endanger my loved ones, personal property or future through *my actions*. I can admit feeling angry, while rejecting the human desire to let is fester. Letting go is something I must do regularly.

Lord, help me to let go!

THOUGHTS

HOPE

As long as I am alive, there is hope for me. ***THERE IS POWER IN CHOICE!!*** As long as I can choose, the power is available for change. No person is in control of my future. I will not throw hope away because of negative influences. The darkest TODAYS can usher in the brightest TOMORROWS.

Lord, help me to hold out!

THOUGHTS

PERSEVERANCE

There are days, I don't want to get out of the bed. Facing the world is not on the agenda for the day. I want to hide from my problems and pretend that they don't exist. I want to lose my thoughts in imagination for a few days. I feel like I cannot go on. *Lord, help me to understand that running and hiding don't bring change.* Help me to accept mistakes and the clean-up that goes with it.

THOUGHTS

PARENTING

Children are quite a responsibility. They require my time and attention. They also depend upon my planning, training, and provisions for their lives. I don't have to feel guilty if I'm not a perfect parent. Nobody is perfect. But I can commit to being unselfish with my time and resources for their benefit. *Lord, show me how to be a selfless parent.*

THOUGHTS

PEACE

Peacemakers reap peace. I want to be at peace with my enemies, friends, family members, co-workers, in-laws, ex's, everybody. Grudges, hatred and strife add unnecessary weight and pressure to my life. Hate is not a word for me. I can give up my right to be right for the sake of positive emotions. *Lord, show me how to become a peacemaker.* Show me how to make peace with the most difficult individuals in my life.

THOUGHTS

PRIDE

There is no reason for me to look down on other people. My circumstances can change in the blink of an eye. Who is to say that what I possess or how I am today will sustain for tomorrow? In a desperate moment, will I not reach out to *another person* for help? I have much in common with others; apart from social, financial, or marital status. *Lord, don't let me be arrogant.* Show me if I'm too judgmental or self-centered.

THOUGHTS

JOY

I don't have to look far to increase the joy in my life.
Service to mankind is plenty. Bringing happiness,
assistance, and provision into the lives of other people
is the ultimate joy life gives. *Lord, don't let me be too busy
to serve my fellow man.* Help me to think of ways to be
a blessing. And don't let me forget the joy
that it will bring me.

THOUGHTS

DISCIPLINE

Discipline will strengthen my soul. Discipline sets a standard for my personal life and home. Discipline sets a good example for my children. Discipline will help me live longer. Discipline invites peace and joy into my space. Discipline can be a decision maker in my life.
Lord, I want to discipline to rule me.

THOUGHTS

INTEGRITY

When I speak, it should make a difference. What I say should be regarded as truth and not a lie. I don't need to say things in a hurry, out of emotion, or to impress others. My word should be my bond. Deliberately using words to deceive, manipulate or control will only come back to haunt me in the end. Speaking and making verbal commitments should be well thought about. Think before you speak is still a good rule. There is a time to speak and a time to keep silent.

Lord, help me to know the difference.

THOUGHTS

LONGSUFFERING

Today was a trying day. I had to suffer; for a long time…The boss was acting crazy, the bank teller wasn't pleasant, The gas station attendant was impatient, The hair salon was overbooked, My neighbors blasted their music, and The children were rebellious. *Lord, give me the strength to endure through the frustrations in life.*

THOUGHTS

QUITTING

Quitting does not become me. I want to start and finish whatever the task at hand. My life is full of unfinished projects. Quitting is no longer an option. None of my goals will be reached without hard work, sacrifice, and some disappointments. What becomes of the life a quitter? Someone living with many regrets. *Lord, don't let me become a person living with many regrets.* Give me the courage not to QUIT.

THOUGHTS

JEALOUSY

Jealousy makes me repeat things about people I shouldn't. Sometimes, I am the catalyst for lies. Gossip and strife are a part of my past time. My actions show I'm jealous, even if my mouth never says a word. I show it by mistreating, ignoring, or exalting myself in the presence of others. *Lord, help me to get past this deep insecurity.* It has weighed me down long enough; and it weighs down other people when I start talking. Help!

THOUGHTS

SELF-ESTEEM

There are many things I can do to build myself up on the inside. I need to building up the part of me hidden from others. That part down deep below the nice clothes, outward swagger, or pasted smile. I often neglect it because it is not readily visible to others, but it has a profound effect on my life choices. I've got to dedicate more time to improving self-concept. *Lord, I need to spend more time working on me.*
Help me make it a priority.

THOUGHTS

CHANGE

I need a change in the way I see things, do things, and the reasoning behind them both. I want freedom from the mundane and the normal. *If I want something I've never had, I've got to do something I've never done. Lord, change is the essence of what you're about.* Change and re-arrange. You're in charge!

THOUGHTS

GREED

I am grateful for the income I have. I won't complain about what I don't. I won't be caught down in the dumps. My decision is a conscious one; no focusing on the negative, but focusing on the positive. I won't keep my eyes on the possessions of others. Envy and jealousy will not change my financial condition.
Lord, help me to stay grateful.

THOUGHTS

FEAR

Fear is not a catalyst for dreams. It hinders any leaps of faith. It cripples any belief in making them reality. There is nothing that can be done about the past, we're living in the present, and only the future can be shaped by our choices.

Lord, free me from fear!

THOUGHTS

INSECURITY

I want to be in a healthy relationship one day. Or I want to maintain the one that I'm in. Pain and hurt from the past caused me to put up emotional. They are thick, and I live behind them. I wear many masks to keep them intact. Loving freely is difficult. I don't bother to tell the other person, which eventually causes conflict. I know it will; but I take my chances. *Lord, help me to stop hiding behind the walls and abandon my selfishness.*

THOUGHTS

PRIDE

Admitting where I fall short is part of maturing. I don't have to be ashamed of my mistakes. My pride won't get in the way of my growth. I won't let my emotions cover them up. God won't let me have a superior attitude about myself; I get caught too much. That is only to prevent a big fall down the road. *Lord, thank you for caring enough about me to let me get caught sometimes.* It's a lifesaver!

THOUGHTS

PROBLEMS

The dog needs to go to the vet…
We need to move out of this house…
Foreclosure found us this year….
We can't afford college….
The car needs to be fixed ….
We got another baby coming….
Our loved one is very ill…
Can't find a job after 2 years…
Lord, none of these are in my control. My list continues and
I continue to turn them over to you.

THOUGHTS

MEDITATION

Silence is golden. When I'm not talking I'm a better listener; to people and to God. I even seem more knowledgeable when I'm not doing all the talking. Silence, combined with privacy cultivates a peaceful space. We all need mental clearing. Our lives are cluttered with responsibilities each day. *Lord, remind me of the importance of stopping and listening to you.*

THOUGHTS

PARENTING

I love my children. I am willing to sacrifice my time, talent, money, and desires to provide for them. I know that my reward is great. Selfishness is a part of human nature, but I resist it. I place my children as first priority and refuse to move them. Any person that enters my life, will always take a backseat. My children will not have space to accuse me of neglecting them in their youth.

Lord, help me never to neglect or abandon my children.

I want their trust always.

THOUGHTS

TIME

Time stands still for no man. I need to use time to my advantage through various investments: education, stocks, bonds, savings, child-rearing, homeownership and community service. Time is on my side when used wisely, and not allowed to *run out on me. Lord, help me to UNDERSTAND THE IMPORTANCE OF TIME MANAGEMENT.*

THOUGHTS

CREATIVITY

Creativity can be the key to a great entrepreneurial opportunity. If I can create, I can buy and sell. I can invent and improve. I can develop and distribute. A whole new world is available to me because of creativity. I embrace it now as a strength, precious gift, and boundless reward. *Lord, show me the many ways to utilize my creativity.* Show me it's power to the change my life.

THOUGHTS

HOPE

HOPE is daily strength in the midst of adversity. The belief that change and newness will find me in this journey, keeps me actively engaged in life. I will not let go of my HOPE. I will not throw it away, let someone steal it, or let my mind be manipulated to abandon it. There are those who desire to steal it from me or stop me from believing in it.

Lord, help me to remain hopeful.

THOUGHTS

BROKEN HEARTED

My heart is broken. My emotions are up and down. When I wake in the morning, my thoughts are about my pain. The one who broke my heart is not here, but I see them in my imagination. Can I handle the rejection? Can I handle the disappointment? Yes I can handle it, because I know in time, my heart will change. *Lord, I know this is just a season.* Preserve me until the next one comes.

THOUGHTS

DISCIPLINE

I want to reap from a life of discipline. I want to eat the fruit of consistency, steadfastness, and focus. *Lord, show me how to have the discipline of a soldier.*

THOUGHTS

PEACE

I deserve to have peace. My home should be peaceful. My car should be peaceful. My workspace, place of worship, family relationships, social networks, and overall daily leaving should be peaceful. *I can have problems and remain peaceful.* Letting go of everything not within my control, will fortify peace in my mind. Making good choices will do the same. Any person, place, or thing that does not bring peace, is not for me.
Lord, show me my personal path of peace.

THOUGHTS

GREED

I should be busy managing my money. Being a good money manager requires my full attention. I need to keep a close eye on the budget, savings, investments, and loose spending. Maybe new habits can change the current situation. Saving is not a dirty word. Spending never takes the place of inner healing. And a good budget will only be to my benefit. *Lord, help me to keep a close eye on the finances placed in my care.* Blind me to the financial business of others.

THOUGHTS

F.E.A.R.

FEAR is a bad word...

F. alse

E. experiences

A. ppearing

R. eal

Lord, let nothing else disturb my peace. Let nothing else hamper my forward momentum. Let all my hindrances disappear.

THOUGHTS

EXCERPT
WAR FOR YOUR
DREAMS

WAR
\WOR\ N.

1
ANY ACTIVE HOSTILITY
OR STRUGGLE

2
MILITARY OPERATIONS
AS A SCIENCE

D.R.E.A.M.S.

DARING

REALIZATIONS

EVOLVING

AND

MANIFESTING

SHAMELESSLY

"Getting pregnant early is like postponing a worldwide expedition.. indefinitely."

Katrina Robinson

Teen Pregnancy War

With my mother working, in college for the 2nd time, and playing catch up in her personal life, I was watching my sisters after school. I did a horrible job with the big sister thing. Boys had my attention now because they gave me attention. I was walking home from school with them, paging them, dating them. When I couldn't get out of the house, I was on the phone with them. Trouble and hardship knocked on the door and I let them in.

Neighborhood boys are the closest ones to get hooked up with. You can conveniently see them when you're bored, broke, or lonely. They're always nearby to sneak around with. The next thing is to start experimenting sexually. Along with that may come alcohol abuse, drug dealing or crime. Idle time can yield a lot of stuff. Costly decisions are easily made when you're immature. One of those is unprotected sex. All of a sudden, pregnancy emerges. An unplanned one. Unplanned pregnancy had found me. After feeling sick for a few days, I decided to get a pregnancy test. I went to Planned Parenthood. I didn't tell anyone, I wanted to go alone. It was a little scary but I had to know. The test was positive. My stride was much slower when I left the facility than when I went in. That kind of news will slow a anybody down. Man, oh Man. The bus trip from that building back home seemed like a lifetime. My mind was racing and my heart was beating fast. Of course I told my two best friends. They just looked at me, but they pledged their support. I felt like daaag...everybody is having sex, but I got caught. I had to tell the father. When he found out, he was not happy. Looking back, I guess that's understandable since we were both high school students. Neither of us was mature at that point. But I never expected him to desert us. Being abandoned was the farthest thing from my mind. I really thought he would do the right thing after he got over the anger or when the baby was born. He never did. I never thought about how much pain I would be in if he disappeared. His family hurt me to my heart. Around my 2nd month of pregnancy, I saw his mother in the grocery store and she was so nasty to me. She was convinced I was on a mission to destroy her son's life. (He obviously had played no part in me getting pregnant!) She almost ran me over in her Chevrolet another day. She stopped in the middle of the street, got out of her car, and started yelling and screaming. Of course she turned a deaf ear to anything I had to say. It was all about him not getting into trouble with the law. Her message very clear. *Abort that baby!* Maybe to her that was the best thing to do, but I was so overwhelmed I couldn't decide what to do. Even abortions cost money and her son had completely cut me off. She took my phone number and vowed to help pay for the procedure. I never heard from her ever again. I started thinking more and more about having an abortion. At the time, I was working at McDonalds. I started saving money for a procedure. Good ole' mom. Most women know when someone is pregnant. They know the signs. She saw how I was laying around all the time. Hiding in my room. Ducking her out. Women are not stupid! "Katrina, are you pregnant?" she asked. "No." I knew I was lying and so did she. She was in my room one day and found the abortion money. She put a stop to that abortion nonsense. She did not support abortion in the least. I'm so glad someone stopped me from making a terrible mistake. The whole ordeal was scary and oh so painful, but I'm glad I went through it.

When delivery time came, I was at the hospital alone. The baby's father didn't come, his family didn't come, and my sisters were too young to make it. My mom came when I went in for surgery. I was laying in the hospital bed and all of a sudden all the wall monitors started going off. My mother called the doctors in. They came rushing in, yelling at each other and moving fast. They adjusted and rolled my bed out of the room. I said, "What's wrong, what's wrong?" None of the doctors would answer me. I guess they figured I was just another kid pregnant before her time and I wouldn't understand anyway. I started crying. I was scared to death. Is the baby dying? How much pain will I be in? My son was having fetal distress (difficulty breathing while inside the womb). They had to rush me in for a C-section. That meant a permanent scar and a long recovery. My mom had to stand outside the operating room because of sterilization. I looked around the room and I was surrounded by strangers. Nobody in there knew me, and I knew none of them. My body was exposed, I was in pain, and an emotional wreck. I just couldn't stop crying. During birth, I was sick to my stomach. I probably vomited at least 5 times that day. Fear overtook me and I didn't have a soul to lean on. The nurse who came to comfort me and hold my hand was no consolation to me. She was a stranger too. All I could do was lie on that table and recall the promises my boyfriend made. I had flashbacks of bad memories too. I was so glad when surgery was over. My son was finally born. I was wheeled back to my room afterward, but I lost a lot of blood. I couldn't even stand up the next day without fainting. I almost killed the nurse that tried to break my fall. She fell too. I stayed in the hospital for a few days. My boyfriend never contacted me. I just gave up on his father and decided it's me and the baby. He was so precious at birth. All babies are. Holding my son helped me forget about some of the pain. He was as the bible would say "a goodly child". Strong, healthy, and cute as a button. His father missed out on that.

We had visitors. A lot of visitors. That helped me emotionally. My best friends gave me a baby shower and the people showered us with gifts. When I got home, I knew I had quite a journey ahead of me. The diaper bags were cute, the baby clothes were cuter, but there was nothing cute about what I was getting ready to face. The responsibility was hitting me like a ton of bricks. It was time for me to start my single parenting journey like many I knew: unstable home, food stamps, Medicaid, child support and on and on. I bounced back from surgery pretty quickly. My son brought joy into the family. He had such personality and was playful as all get out. I was a scared little sister getting ready to be made a strong sister for real.

The town we lived in was very small. Everybody knew everybody. Nobody had private life secrets. I got tired of being asked questions about the baby and his father. My mother didn't help. Everything she knew, she told someone, that told someone, that told someone. I guess she had to vent to somebody. Unfortunately, my life was on blast for about 2 years. This was especially shameful because I was striving so hard to make things better. I could never live down my mistakes; even to people I didn't even know. Filing for child support came with getting cash assistance from social services. My ex's family hid him from the sheriff when they tried to serve court papers. He stopped answering the telephone. All of a sudden, he just disappeared. Nobody has seen him. His family moved him away to escape all the drama and rumors. Lucky him. The baby and I had to stay and live through the mess.

Despite everything, I was determined to finish high school. I was not going to be a dropout. It wasn't easy, but with some help from mom, grandma, friends and three little sisters, I pulled on through. My son was my motivation. I did it for him. *I didn't care enough about myself to do it for me.* Looking at him, it was all worth it. I didn't miss the proms either. The pictures from the junior prom showed my big belly. My father's girlfriend made me a dress to wear. Everybody thought I wouldn't get a date but I did. My friend Walter. He took the pregnant girl to the prom even though the baby wasn't his. What a nice guy. I will never forget that evening. He made it fun for both of us. And we had a good time.

I went to the senior prom too. My father sprung for the most beautiful dress I had ever seen. Baby boy was a year old by then. I took pictures with him before getting in the limousine. In that moment, I forgot about being ugly, dark skinned, or a failure. I actually felt like my life mattered just for one night. Getting a high school diploma was a big hurdle, but I made it. My friends and I celebrated. Now, another WAR had started. The war for my son's dreams. As a teen mother, I was in no position to posture him for a quality life. I couldn't save, invest, teach him foreign languages, or get him heavily involved in early learning. His father was gone, and I was preoccupied. So the cycle continued.

My best friends encouraged me to keep going and apply to college. Having a baby didn't stop my aptitude from working, so I did. I applied to local four year universities. My high school g.p.a. of 3.2 landed me a scholarship to Coppin State. That's right. An academic scholarship covering full tuition and books. No headaches, no long lines to stand in. Everything paid for. I was eligible for the next 3 years of free tuition if I kept my grades up. Unfortunately, I didn't know what I had in my hands.

College was a great experience. Meeting instructors, foreign students, and having the freedom of making up my own mind. It afforded me too much freedom. Cutting classes, playing cards, watching the steppers and going to frat parties was a regular part of my course schedule! Unfortunately, the experience came to an abrupt end with another pregnancy. I still had no self-worth. I had no vision for my life. So when an opportunity presented itself to get involved with another man, I did. I was just ignorant and desperate. This college dude seemed so much better than the last one. We were quite the couple in college. Studying, partying, and even working together. We met each other's family and spent every moment outside of classes together. Oh, how I was deceived. Not by a guy, but because of my own lack of knowledge. I was perishing in ignorance. This good dude had a lot of bad. The "good" was only 1/2 of his life. He had dark secrets I hadn't found out about. They slowly surfaced right before I found out I was pregnant. Man…I was supposed to have found the way this time. I was supposed to have made better choices. But the truth was, my priorities were still wrong and my self-esteem was still in the toilet. This relationship cost me big time. I had to drop out of college and forfeit my scholarship. I had another baby coming. I was so ashamed. I couldn't face my mother. I could barely face my closest friends. And guess what? You got it. My boyfriend disappeared. Now on top of all the negative names I called myself, stupid was added to the list. Nobody helped me with that one. I labeled myself.

Life was like déjà vu. I had just walked this road of struggle and living like a gypsy with my mother. Wrong choices had brought me to the same path. Now, I was the one who needed to borrow a car, chase down bus fare, and find somewhere to live. Actually the cycle had already started in my mind years before. No discipline, no character, no mentor, no God. A path of destruction. It was time to get some skills and find a job. My current skill set was zero. I enrolled in a secretarial program. You know, one of those corner training centers that popped up in the 1980's. That's the least I could do being I was pregnant and all. The center taught data entry, office software, and career management. My stomach was big, but I forced myself to sit at those computer for hours. None of my assignments were missing and I didn't miss any classes. I finished at the top of my class...one of the fastest typist and the highest g.p.a. It was another accomplishment.

My mother threw me out of the house because of my wild lifestyle. Between the guys, lies, late nights, and now another baby; she couldn't take it anymore. (Now that I'm a parent, I realize there does come a point where you have to let go.) Tough love, you can't beat it.

We moved from place to place; living with parents, family members, in a shelter, to living with a guy. I lost possessions with every move. It wasn't a time to try and hold on to anything of sentimental value, and it hurt. We were unstable, and would be for the next few years. I remember living off food stamps, medical assistance, and cash assistance just like my mom did. I remember the low wage jobs, trying to get day care and trying to find a house all at the same time. I remember waking up some days and saying, "I'm so ashamed of myself. What am I going to do? What's going to happen to us?"

My uncle saw me struggling and suggested applying for unemployment. Unemployment benefits? I had never heard of unemployment before. I caught the bus to the unemployment office, and signed up. There was quite a bit of money paid into my insurance. That money carried me for a little while. Renting a house was a first for me, but I had to find one. The townhouses I found were cheap and in the middle of nowhere. *The buses ran once every 2 hours.* It was the cheapest rental I could find. Tidewater Village, I'll never forget that place. My first permanent home away from home. The rental office denied me, but would approve if I had a co-signer. Thank God for my dad. He co-signed so the kids and I could have a roof over our heads.

My second child was born right on schedule. No C-section this time. I had a healthy baby girl by regular birth. She wasn't like her brother, she cried a lot. It didn't bother me any. It's something about motherhood that helps with all the pain and strain. When I left the hospital, I stayed with my mother for a few days to recuperate, then went back to my house. Anyone who came to visit that had a car got the royal treatment. I had one baby on my hip and one baby in the stroller riding the buses to get around. Can you imagine trying to go grocery shopping on the bus with a toddler and an infant in the strollers? Can you imagine the days it was raining? I didn't have enough hands to carry the groceries, stroller, diaper bag, and pocket book. We did a lot of borrowing too. I can see how God kept me from getting hooked on drugs or alcohol. That's all people did out there in those woods was get high, get drunk, and have sex. I still had a made up mind *that I can do better*. My father brought a few pieces of used furniture to start us off. My boyfriend re-appeared for a short time, bought a few things, and then disappeared again. This time, I was ready.

The unemployment job service helped me get a resume together and start applying for clerical jobs. I kept those resumes and applications going out despite deep depression, anxiety and hopelessness.

A community college contacted me for a job as a grant funded part-time secretary position. You talk about excited! That wasn't the word! An interview for a real job – with real benefits. What was I going to wear? None of the money that came through my hands was spent on clothing acceptable for office work. One black dress hung in my closet that covered enough of my body to pass an interview. What would I say? A serious salvage of the memory went on. Attempting to recollect my work experience and communicate it effectively to others would be a challenge. Especially since my brain was so scrambled I could barely remember if I was coming or going. How would I get there? I laid out the connecting bus routes on paper. It took three buses just to get to the daycare. Then a 2-mile walk to the college campus.

6am came quickly the day of the interview. Actually it felt good to have a reason to dress up. A diaper bag packed with diapers and milk was on my shoulder.

Princess was in my arm and baby J was at my knee. In the other hand a stroller, for when my shoulders and back would fail. On the bus off the bus, on the bus off the bus, on the bus off the bus, and then walk to the daycare. Then the 2-mile journey began. The college was two miles from day care and sat on a high hill. I walked from childcare up the hill. So much went through my mind. *They won't hire me. They're going to look at me and know I'm struggling to make it. They're going to laugh at me. Can I answer all the questions? I should just go home.* But one thing stayed on my mind. If didn't go to the interview, my fate would *be sealed* as a statistic. That was not an option. By the time of my arrival on the campus, I needed to rest just from the journey. The interview didn't last long and surprisingly I got hired. I finally landed a job. Happiness is getting hired! A secretarial job was good money compared to an unemployment check. It was at a college with health benefits, retirement, pre-tax plans, and credit union options. Being gainfully employed changes your whole life. I found out my new employer even paid for college tuition. Wow! A second chance at a college education was more than I could imagine.

I could see a dim light at the end of a long tunnel. Then the *real* challenges began. Getting up everyday at 6am, riding all the buses and then walking to work. Then doing the same thing to get home, whether it rained, thundered, or snowed. Snow and ice bruised my feet as I carried the kids on and off the buses. It was hardest on the days when Princess and Baby J did not cooperate. They had days when they slowed me down crying, whining, or not wanting to get off the bus when it was time. I stayed skinny those years. I had plenty of daily exercise. I'd get blessed sometimes with a ride by one of my co-workers. The money I made part-time was just enough to replace the social service benefits that were cut. My budget was very strict. My clothes had holes in them, but I ironed them and wore them to work anyway. I went hungry during lunch most of the time, but the joy of having a job kept me going. It was HOPE for the future. Some days I would just cry. Wondering when would things get better? *I cried and kept pushing. I was ashamed, but I kept pushing. Thinking about suicide, but I kept pushing.* Some days it would rain on us so hard on the bus stop. God forbid there was a storm with high winds. Sometimes, I just stayed at daycare and made my journey later on in the evening. Often, I would forget it was the 1st day of the month and my bus pass would be expired. I didn't know what day of the week it was most days. I would have to get off the bus and go buy a new bus pass. Some days we had to run for the bus. Other days the bus would leave us and we had to wait an hour for the next one. Every now and then, the bus didn't even show up! And rarely, I'd treat myself to a hacker or taxi. I cried a lot during those days and nobody heard my cries but God.

I finally got a car and started gaining forward momentum. Someone told me about car auctions and I saved enough to show up and take a chance. Without any idea what I was doing, I bid on a two door hatchback 1989 Renault Alliance. Few people bid against me that day so it was mine! It cost $500. *I shouted every day for a year.* No more two mile walks, strollers, taxis, begging for rides, heavy grocery bags, and bus transfers. Life was getting better. I would definitely get my money's worth even if the car just lasted for 3 months.

My clerical position was grant funded so I had to look for another job close to the end of the grant. (We'll talk more about this first job later.) I applied for a full-time job on campus as a clerk-typist. They hired me 2 weeks after the interview. *(Later, I found out I got the job because no one else applied.)* I started thinking it was Christmas. I had a full time salary, good benefits and good credit. After that, it was back to school to finish the Accounting program. Thank God for aptitude! Working and going to college was a challenge, but being young helped a lot in that respect. I started working on my education while the kids were young which turned out to be rewarding. (That's my advice to all teen parents. Get your education while they are babies because you're going to need a good job and a flexible schedule when they become teens. That's another book....)

The engine on my Renault blew because I didn't know about oil changes. My best friend's father had to come and get my car out of the middle of the street. It broke down during rush hour at a major intersection. I had traffic backed up for miles. I had no notion of car maintenance so I learned the hard way. I started spoiling myself. I upgraded my car to a Mazda 626. My first car payment! Now I was beginning to build up some credit. I got rid of those worn clothes and bought everything new. Time to look professional! I bought some suits and heels for work. I moved closer to civilization in another townhouse. No co-signer needed! I had income. My grandmother was nearby and provided daycare for the kids. Going to the beauty salon, shopping, and pedicures became routine. It felt good after all the pain I had been through. I really started to feel better about myself. I stopped running from the mirror. Now that I was on my own, I grew into some new relationships with other women. We started building each other up and sharing resources. My kids were being provided for without me begging for help. I was doing better than many of the people who laughed at me. Not that I cared, I just wanted to stop riding all those buses. The kids brought me much joy. My son's personality was calm, cool, and collected – just like he is now. He was spoiled too. I always bought him solid turtle necks with striped sweaters over top and jeans. That was his signature outfit. He just looked so dapper. My daughter was still whiny, but she changed a whole lot after age 6. (Funny, she got whiny again at 17). I was so sick of Chucky Cheese, but they loved it. For a short time, I even had them in Catholic school to make sure they got the best education possible. Both of them were supportive and my driving force to keep on going.

After finishing my Associates degree, I found a four year college that had onsite child care. I still wanted to get that Bachelor's degree. I got bold! The sense of accomplishment I had, and everything that came with it felt good. I wanted more. I needed more. My children were counting on me to provide and help them. I took it very seriously.

Chapter Two

THE

ROOTS

UGLY is not a bad word...

U.

G. otta

L. ove

Y. ourself

Katrina Robinson

YOU'RE UGLY

There was a time in the 1980's where it was very popular to be light skinned. Being dark skinned didn't mean you were ugly, but light skinned girls received a lot more attention than the darker. I think this was partly attributed to young female images in the media during those years. They were usually brown to light skinned with long hair. (or a weave) I was totally opposite. My skin was fairly dark and my hair was naturally short. To make matters worse, my bottom lip was discolored from birth – like I had been smoking. Those teen years probably wouldn't have been as bad if "you're ugly" hadn't been fed to me as a child.

When the Jeri Curl came out, my mother took me to the beauty salon to get one. The jeri curl wouldn't take properly because my hair was too "nappy". My mom and the beautician laughed at me. "We don't know what kind of hair you got. It must be African." At the age of 10, you can only sit there and stare, but inwardly, there was definitely a deposit. My self-image was being tampered with.

My parents adopted me and had other kids not far after. My mother was a brown skinned woman who was scorned by my father. He cheated on her constantly. He left her with 4 kids and she barely could to take care of us. Can you guess what kind of women he cheated on her with? You got it. Dark skinned women. Every woman he dated was dark skinned and had strong personalities. Growing up, my strong personality started developing and our relationship didn't get any better. I was naturally outgoing, a risk taker, intelligent, and popular with the fellas. I gave her hell with all the guys calling and coming to the house. I also believe deep inside, I represented everything she wanted to be as a person, but she just wasn't built that way. As an adoptee, with my father gone, mom and I never really "connected". The love and support she gave to the others I did not receive. I believe some of this is natural, but some of it was pure hatred. I reminded her of all those women my father had left her to run behind.

Her only expression of this anger and jealousy was to remind me of my "faults"..my pink lip, short hair, dark skin, and just plain old "ugly" self. She reminded me constantly of how dark my skin was. It was always made a point that my skin was too dark to wear the color red. Red just didn't look right on somebody of my shade. She told me that my bottom lip looked like a monkey's behind. Any quality relationships with men that came my way, she made sure they got destroyed before they started.

As I got older and recalled all the slurs, lack of support, and cruel treatment I recognized it was hatred in her heart. You know how I know? I have my own daughter whom I love dearly. I could never say or do those things to my child. The only way that I could, is if we were disconnected and I was jealous of something about her.

That's how I know. Love would not do such things to one of its own.

For all you teenagers out there I can tell you it is a waste of time to work tirelessly trying to like somebody else. It never works. Be the most beautiful YOU possible, regardless of the opinions of other people. Don't allow others to define your beauty. That is your responsibility. That begins when you take that look in the mirror. If you are satisfied, be happy with it. If not, it's o.k. to apply make-up, creams, or treatments. But all these surgeries are dangerous! I always say if it requires surgery, I don't need it. IT IS NOT THAT DEEP.

I know many of you have been called "ugly" by people. Others of you have been called "ugly" by more than one person so it really damaged your self-concept. So, some of you accepted that the fact that you are "ugly" instead of declaring **WAR FOR YOUR DREAMS**. "Ugly" has been infused into your lifestyle. Some of you hate what you see in the mirror because of SOMEONE ELSE'S opinion. Not because it's what's true. Who defines what's true? *YOU DO*. It's that simple. Once you declare yourself beautiful, a fox, too hot to handle, all of that you are. It's all in attitude. It doesn't take surgery, or trying to look like a celebrity, or even copying someone in your close circle. It's a state of mind. Refusing to take pictures, care for your body properly, looking your best at all times, and having sex with anybody who calls you "pretty" are signs of low-self esteem.

Being called "ugly" does hurt. It does make you want to

change your appearance to stop the mean words coming your way. But we live in a cold, cruel world. Somebody somewhere will always have something negative to say about you even if it has nothing to do with your looks. You will not escape criticism. Someone will always be jealous or hateful towards you. Expect for your feelings to be hurt. *The key is, knowing the person who said it to you may well have pain of their own to process.* IT HAS NOTHING TO DO WITH YOU. Their comments towards you are an outward sign of their personal inward problem. I can't tell you the number of people I know that have titles, positions, influence and money, but still have negative self-image. You can always tell because they exhibit very cruel behavior towards people. Most often they look down on people, valuing them based on status, power and money; not on character content. Don't carry anybody else's burdens.

The person who called you "ugly" just may not want to see you happy or empowered. Miserable people who know inwardly that they are not going anywhere in life want lots of company. So tearing you down is easier than pushing you to fly.

As the years went by, I learned something......

A lot of men love dark skinned women

Short hair makes great hairstyles

I look great in red, and other colors for that matter

And my pink lip doesn't even matter

See, the slurs were illusions to trick me into thinking less of myself. They were planted in my mind to destroy my self-image. They were a driving force behind bad decisions I made. Ultimately, they were distractions to stop me from pursuing my dreams.

Don't let anything kill your dreams!

EVERYTHING is *ALWAYS* up for grabs.

Katrina Robinson

YOU'LL NEVER BE NOTHING!

The next time someone says that to you respond with all boldness, "THAT'S A LIE AND I DON'T RECEIVE IT." Then put it behind you. They may look at you funny but say it again so they know you mean it. The person speaking those words knows assuredly that they have no clue what your future holds. Treat them like they don't. SEIZE THE MOMENT TO STOP NEGATIVITY IN ITS TRACKS. People who say things like that need help that you cannot give. They obviously have no regard for your feelings, worth or desires. Understand that. They are speaking from a realm that they have no knowledge of....your future. See it for what it is.. a **WAR** tactic to complicate your life.

You can't afford to absorb that into your emotional system. Those words are full of poison. Would you drink a poisonous drink if you knew it would kill you? Certainly not. Then you should treat negative words with the same tenacity and attitude. Don't allow someone else's negative perspective about your future BECOME YOURS. The battle for a long, fulfilling life is already over if it is counted as over with before it even starts.

Hearing this as a child can be painful and lingering.

Hearing it for the first time at any age can be shocking. It may leave you wondering where did that come from? Was it something you did? Is there any truth to it? Not necessarily. I told you before; people have all kinds of motives for doing and saying negative things. Some people hate themselves so much, their mission in life is to make other people miserable. Unfortunately, they really don't see anything wrong with it. They rationalize it as expressing their opinion. Or maybe "just trying to give you a dose of reality". Well, when it comes to negativity, you have the right to ask them not to. Your self-esteem, self-image, and confidence are not tangible. They are housed among your mental and emotional faculties. But they can still be damaged parallel to being shot, stabbed, or clobbered. If somebody attacked you physically, I'm quite sure you would defend yourself to the fullest. The same is with negativity. Defend and fight diligently.

As awful as these words are to hear, they can be used as fuel for future goals. Let the anger, frustration, embarrassment, and sheer humiliation you feel compel you to prove the individual wrong. Become compelled to live life to the fullest. It's not against the rules to harbor the memories *IF THEY DRIVE YOU TOWARD BECOMING BETTER.* This by the way is also a **WAR** tactic. One that works to your benefit.

If you make them sick, they probably already were.

Katrina Robinson

YOU MAKE ME SICK

Within the context of being made sick outside of some physical condition, an individual shouldn't be made to feel like a walking air born pathogen. In other words, being told "you make me sick" implies that the mere sight of or dealing with you brings a repulsive feeling. It can't feel good for that to be part of your identity. Especially when it's driven by another person's anger, lashing out, jealous rage, or bouts of self-deception. For example, teens being told they "make someone sick" because they are "just like their father/mother". Well, if two people come together and have a child, the child will have traits of one or both of the parents. It's a little unfair to view them as "sickening" for being what was produced genetically. The child had no control over that.

I made my mother sick because of her own personal notions of my having sexual feelings toward my father. Although he was abusive to my mother, he treated me like a normal dad should. He never did or said anything perverted to me. I was his daughter. (And he didn't mind handing out whippings). On more than one occasion, she accused me of trying to be with him or gain his attention in the wrong way. That's an example of self-deception. A person is not concerned about the truth, they have adopted their own. Don't bother trying to having discussions or "set the record straight". There's no telling what is really driving their thoughts.

If you are around people who you make sick, the best thing you can do is get away. Usually "you make me sick" comes from someone you have a relationship with: family member or significant other. Yes, even husband and wives hear this phrase from the very person who made vows to them and crawls into bed with them at night. The phrase is usually driven by historical knowledge. The person speaking is aware of your pattern of actions and attitudes. There is nothing you can do about other people's bad memories, broken heart, suspicions, or inner pain. And you are not supposed to. We are all responsible for our own decisions, actions, and motives. Don't take "you make me sick" with you along life's journey. You may be the very treatment needed for someone else's inner ailments.

RE-ORDER:

www.authorhouse.com

LEAVE COMMENTS :

www.twitter.com/warforyourdream

For speaking engagements, billing, or other information
visit online:
www.povertytopotential.com

www.facebook.com/povertytopotential

THOUGHTS

THOUGHTS

THOUGHTS